MICHELANGELO

MICHELANGELO

BY MARC LE BOT

CROWN TRADE PAPERBACKS · NEW YORK

Title page: PRESUMED SELF-PORTRAIT OF MICHELANGELO
The Figure of Nicodemus in PIETÀ, ca 1550
Marble, height 89˝ (226 cm) detail
Cathedral, Florence
Photo Scala, Florence

Series published under the direction of:
MADELEINE LEDIVELEC-GLOECKNER

Translated from the French by:
MARIE-HÉLÈNE AGÜEROS

Published by Crown Trade Paperbacks, 201 East 50th Street, New York, New York 10022.
Member of the Crown Publishing Group.

Random House, Inc. New York, Toronto, London, Sydney, Auckland

CROWN TRADE PAPERBACKS and colophon are trademarks of Crown Publishers, Inc.
Originally published in hardcover by Crown Publishers, Inc., in 1992.

Printed in Italy - Poligrafiche Bolis S.P.A., Bergamo

Library of Congress Cataloging-in-Publication is available upon request.

ISBN 0-517-88375-9

10 9 8 7 6 5 4 3 2 1

First Paperback Edition

TONDO DONI
THE HOLY FAMILY
WITH SAINT-JOHN THE BAPTIST AS A CHILD
ca 1504
Distemper on panel, 47 ¹/₄" (120 cm) in diameter
The Uffizi Gallery, Florence
Photo Nicolò Orsi Battaglini, Florence

Philosopher Holding a Skull, ca 1490. Pen, yellowish-brown and grayish brown ink
13" × 8 1/2" (33.1 × 21.5 cm). The British Museum, London. Malcolm Collection

Michelangelo was a painter, as well as a sculptor and an architect. He practiced the three arts of space and excelled in everyone of them. This treble achievement remains unparalleled, whether in his or any other time. That these three arts could be mastered by a single artist, and that Michelangelo had the intellectual strength to practice all three of them, does not necessarily mean that he was a better artist, but it points to a crucial problem in the culture of his time: A new conception of space was at stake. Man had to reconsider the space of his physical world and, also, his own mental space. By working in the three arts, Michelangelo showed that his preoccupations and thoughts as an artist were attuned to contemporary science and technology.

It seems now that modern times were born out of the industrial revolution which started in the eighteenth century. This revolution reorganized the order of time in the life of society. It changed and quickened the pace and the connections between productive activities. These innovations, however, would not have been possible without a new concept of space, its measurement and symbolic order, which was defined four hundred years earlier, when fourteenth-century Italy underwent a renaissance in science and art. By the sixteenth century, this issue of the concept and representation of space had reached a sort of peak, which was expressed with particular brilliance in Michelangelo's work. Before people could master their time, they needed to take possession of their world and acquire a better knowledge of their world's place in the universe.

As for the discovery and conquest of the earth and its roundness, the men who made the transition from the fifteenth to the sixteenth century were representative of the new perspectives opened up to European societies. Michelangelo was twenty years younger than Christopher Columbus and five years older than Ferdinand Magellan. He belonged, however, to the family of minds who elaborated the notions which were to make it possible to survey and later conquer the earth. He belonged to a line of fifteenth-century painters of perspective. They were among the first to work toward the construction of a strict system of Euclidian geometry, thus contributing to a "realistic" representation of space, but also to a relevant system of measurements which remains applicable to this day.

As for a general concept of universal space which gave mankind and earth a place which was then fiercely challenged, Michelangelo belonged to the time of Copernicus and Galileo. In this field there was no overlap — not even a temporary one — between the philosophy of science and that of the arts, as there was one in the field of geometry. But the three-dimensional space conceived by painters, sculptors, and architects would present such imaginary shapes as the ellipse, which appeared in geometric figures and celestial mechanics, often unbeknownst to the scientists. The real complicity between science and art lay in the formal models built from a similar orientation in the imagination of artists and scientists. In the intellectual and social adventure which led the Europeans to "become the masters and owners of nature," as René Descartes put it one century later, the role of the arts, unlike that of science and technology, could not be assessed from its practical consequences. If it is true, however, that art, and the philosophy of art, is as significant to the mind as science, then Michelangelo was not the mere contemporary of Copernicus and Galileo. His role was similar to theirs, inasmuch as he discovered a modern approach to space, its measurements and, more importantly, its symbolic order.

What is it that we call "space"? Does "space" exist? It is not a physical object, it is not even a reality which can be perceived like objects. Italian painters of the early Renaissance created a system of spatial measurements which they called "perspective." Thus they undid the old hierarchical order by which the medieval mind could conceive of the relationship between people and things in a space where they coexisted. The definitions of this relationship, as they were established first during the Renaissance, then during the classical period — the so-called modern times — did not last much longer, at least not theoretically. Modern science has overturned the concepts of space and time as they were established in earlier centuries, especially the relationship by which one was seen as a function of the other. The concept of spatial relationship in contemporary art could be expressed in terms of a metaphorical topology: terms of inclusion and exclusion, proximity and distance, attraction and repulsion. And they give pride of place to serial and combinative logic, as does music. This implies other symbolic connections, other relationships between people, and between people and objects, which call to mind an imaginary resemblance to some scientific notions: These relationships are viewed as dominated by an ambivalence similar to that created by topological connections and serial games.

Michelangelo's work shows that these modern ideas about the creation of forms, which are characteristic of both the arts and science of the same culture, have their source in the works of the Renaissance artists. From this point of view, Michelangelo's work cannot be separated from that of his contemporaries. The works of Leonardo da Vinci, Giorgione, Titian, and Raphael belong to the same intellectual movement and their contribution is no less significant than that of Michelangelo's. What sets Michelangelo's work apart was that it developed simultaneously in the three visual arts. It points to the unity of the artist's perception of space within a culture, through its structural, symbolic, and decorative orders. Michelangelo created the decoration of places of high spirituality, such as the Sistine Chapel. He created figures symbolizing the philosophical ideas of his time, such as his *David* and his *Moses*. He worked on the architectural design of major buildings, such as Saint Peter's Basilica in Rome. In the same spirit, he designed urban plans, such as the Piazza del Campidoglio and the opening of the avenue leading to Porta Pia. His concept of space and its unity throughout his work reach a great level of abstraction. One could say that Michelangelo was a philosopher artist. He did not separate his experience of human reality from a reflection on the structure of the physical world, nor, especially at the end of his life, from a meditation on man's fate, which he expressed in his poetry as well as in the visual arts. Giorgio Vasari published in 1550, and again in 1568, his "Lives of the Best Italian Painters, Sculptors, and Architects." He claimed that the Italian Renaissance in the arts started with Giotto (1266/1267-1337) and reached its peak with that which he called Michelangelo's "terribilità". This word became famous, and understandably so. It evokes man's fear and tremor as he strives in his mind to embrace, as best as he can, the space of the earth on which he lives, the interstellar universe, and that which could be called the time-space of his destiny.

When the fourteen-year-old Michelangelo (1475-1564) started working in Domenico Ghirlandajo's studio (1449-1494), he was already something of an *enfant terrible*. Contemporary fashion in Florence favored the seductive style of Filippino Lippi (1457-1504), Sandro Botticelli (1445-1510), as well as Domenico Ghirlandajo. Two red-chalk drawings made by Michelangelo in the latter's studio are extant, as well as copies of figures painted by Masaccio (1401-1428) around 1425 in the Brancacci Chapel of the Carmine Church in Florence. It is also known that among Michelangelo's early works, there were drawings after figures from Giotto's frescoes. From the very beginning, the young boy made himself independent of the master who was teaching him his art, and also of the style dominant in Florence at the time. He even took the opposite course. The figures painted by Botticelli and Lippi evoked an art that idealized the human body by combining curves and counter-curves for the outlines, and almost flat tints for the surface of the bodies. Michelangelo copied Giotto and Masaccio and chose to render the relief, the massive build of bodies, and he used *chiaroscuro* to mold the heavy folds of the cloaks covering the figures. For reasons which are both visual and intellectual, this effect of weight and mass — one could almost say of gravity — is on a par with another gravity, that of the expression on the faces he drew. The faces are seamed with lines of age, and their stillness suggests mental concentration and depth of thoughts.

Three Standing Figures
after Masaccio, 1501-1503?
Pen and sepia ink, 11³/₈" × 7³/₄" (29 × 19.7 cm)
Albertina, Vienna. Photo Bildarchiv der
Österreichischen Nationalbibliothek

Taking Giotto as a model, the young Michelangelo turned to an art of painting in which Vasari had rightly seen the origins of the Italian Renaissance. Giotto was the first thinker of our humanist culture, before the philosophers, albeit not before the poets. Our whole modern culture was to be born from this original humanism, not only in the arts, but also in the sciences and, more generally, in our social order. Giotto started to paint his frescoes at Assisi in 1290 and, around 1305, those in the Scrovegni Chapel in Padua. He depicted the lives of Saint Francis and Christ with human figures in action. They are contradictory actions. From its inception, the greatness of the humanist philosophy lay in its concept of man as the agent of his own fate, whereby his actions pit him against other men and he directs his actions against the matter of things, so that it is he who changes the face of the world; therefore, the meaning given to the world's reality should be reconsidered in view of man's judgment rather than God's authority. As Michelangelo understood it, Giotto rendered the massive character of the human body, which he draped in heavy cloth and made to resemble a sculpture. His style did not have a lasting following, however, probably because the representation of the space around the figures was stereotyped like a stage set and failed to impart a feeling of depth. Masaccio's genius was to place his figures in an open space, the scale of which fit the strength and motion suggested by the mass and posture of the bodies. This effect was achieved as much, and even more, through the colors, than through the use of linear perspective. And the young Michelangelo may not have been the only artist who often made the pilgrimage to the Brancacci Chapel to find an inspiration in Masaccio's exceptional mastery in the rendition of space.

The earliest known works of Michelangelo addressed the problem of space. At the end of the fifteenth century, the fashion in Florence favored Filippino Lippi's and Sandro Botticelli's style, by which the human body was represented as an outline in the shape of an arabesque. These sinuous lines intertwined with other lines created by the details in the decor. A formal continuity was established, therefore, between the human figure and the space around it: The viewer scanned the picture by moving from line to line, without breaks. By contrast, the young Michelangelo thought in terms of strong oppositions, of mass against mass. He perceived the reality of physical and mental life as made of clashes.

Michelangelo did not stay long in the studio of Ghirlandajo. In 1489, the Duke of Florence, Lorenzo de Medici, took him under his protection. He was accepted at a school located in the garden of the Medici palace in Florence, where the Prince displayed his collection of works from ancient Greece and Rome. Bertoldo di Giovanni, himself a pupil of Donatello (1386-1466), was the director of its school of sculpture. While he was there, Michelangelo made two bas-reliefs in marble, which are extant: *The Madonna of the Stairs* (see p. 13) and *The Battle of the Centaurs* (see p. 11). They are two very different works. *The Madonna of the Stairs* is a static figure, bringing

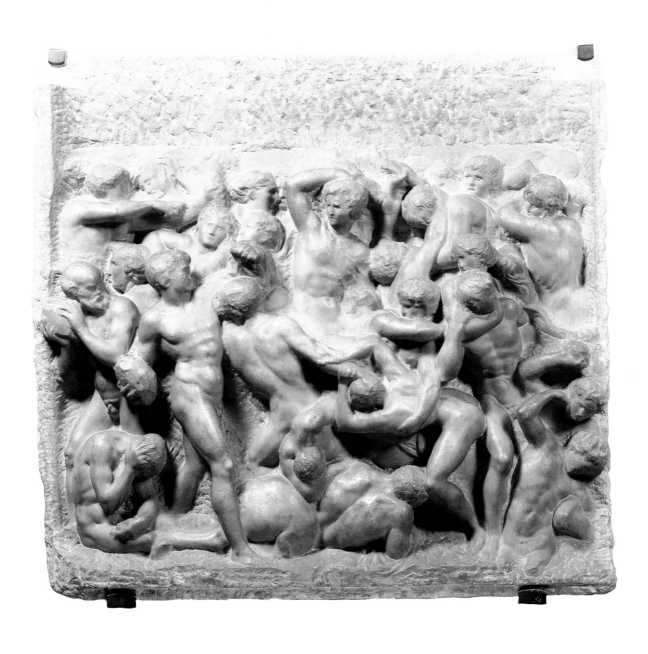

THE BATTLE OF THE CENTAURS, ca 1492
Bas-relief in marble, 35 5/8" × 35 5/8" (90.5 × 90.5 cm)
Casa Buonarroti, Florence
Photo Scala, Florence

11

Tondo Pitti, 1504-1505
Marble, 33 13/16" × 32 1/4" (85.8 × 82 cm)
Bargello, Florence
Photo Nicolò Orsi Battaglini, Florence

THE MADONNA OF THE STAIRS, 1490-1492
Bas-relief in marble, 21 13/16" × 15 3/4" (55.5 × 40 cm)
Casa Buonarroti, Florence
Photo Scala, Florence

to mind those paintings and sculptures in Michelangelo's later work that bear the spirit of meditation. By contrast, *The Battle of the Centaurs* is a tangle of dynamic shapes, evoking later works in which this masterful combination is pushed to the limit, *The Last Judgment* in particular (see p. 63). Characteristically, the bodies remain half caught in the stone, and it is unclear who is fighting against whom in this battle. The work makes a double statement: Man's life is a struggle, a battle with the physical world to which his own body belongs. The young Michelangelo conceived of human space in terms of oppositions and, above all, in terms of meditation and action as two equally necessary components in the life of the mind. The ceiling of the Sistine Chapel was to be a brilliant testimony to this philosophy.

Michelangelo's life, and the conditions under which he worked, were quite eventful and sometimes chaotic. For two years after he left Ghirlandajo's studio, Michelangelo enjoyed a very easy existence. Lorenzo de Medici took notice of him soon after he was accepted as a student in the sculpture school of the Giardino Mediceo. From 1490 to 1492 he lived in the Medici palace. But Lorenzo died in 1492 and Michelangelo was forced to return to his father's modest house. He kept working and made the wooden *Crucifixion* intended for the convent of Santo Spirito (see p. 15). The crucified figure already hinted at the swaying hip motion which became characteristic of his later sculptures. This motion of the body was to express one of his more significant ideas as a painter and sculptor, as well as his perception of the place of the human figure in space.

Michelangelo's life was marked by the increasingly troubled political situation in Florence. Around 1482 Savonarola, a Dominican monk, had started preaching in the church of Santa Maria del Fiore, calling the city to abide more by religious and moral rules. By the year 1490, he had acquired a great following. Troubles had already started in Florence with the plot of the Pazzi against the Medici and, from 1478 to 1480, the war launched against it by the Pope and Sienna. Soon the Medici were temporarily driven out of Florence and replaced by a republic under Savonarola's leadership. Michelangelo expected more serious troubles and he fled the city in October 1494. He spent a year in Bologna after a brief stay in Venice. In December 1495 he returned to Florence because he supported the republican regime and believed that the situation had become relatively calm. He left again in June 1496, this time for Rome, where he hoped to find commissions which he could not get in his native city. And he was to know other troubled periods in his life. These may be the main reasons for a sort of instability, which was not of his choice since, like most artists, he needed a certain peace to be creative. Moreover, the work of a sculptor is a lengthy effort, requiring heavy tools and a large studio. Another reason, however, for this agitation may lie in what is known about his character. His fierce need for independence could drive him to an attitude of intransigence. He offended those who commissioned works from him, as it could be seen from the story of his contentious dealings with Pope Julius II.

CRUCIFIXION OF THE CONVENT OF SANTO SPIRITO, ca 1492. Polychrome wood, 55 7/8" × 53 1/8" (142 × 135 cm)
Casa Buonarroti, Florence. Photo Scala, Florence

Michelangelo was a taciturn and irascible man, but these character traits must be viewed also in the light of the necessity created by the works he sought to make. In the last resort, Michelangelo's character was shaped by this necessity.

He had worked during his stay in Bologna and had made three small statues. In Rome he began a very productive period and created several outstanding works. He remained very productive when he returned to Florence from 1501 until 1505. These years were marked by five major works: the *Pietà* commissioned by Cardinal Jean Bilhères and now standing in Saint Peter's in Rome; the *Madonna* now standing at the Church of Notre-Dame in Bruges; the *David*, which first stood on the Piazza della Signoria in Florence; the tondo of a *Madonna with Child* for Bartolomeo Pitti; and the only wood panel painted by Michelangelo, the tondo of the *Holy Family*, also called *Madonna Doni*. Some of these works present human types which are the most representative of the humanist philosophy. Others are interesting because of the particular placement of these figures in a space.

The *Pietà* (see p. 17) may be famous mostly because of its theme: The grief of a mother crying over her dead child, which may be mankind's deepest grief. It is also famous because Michelangelo smoothed out the agony and made it almost bearable: The Madonna's face is peaceful, her body young. Her posture is also peaceful. The folds in her dress impart a paradoxical motion to this scene of death. The motion of the body, which is barely perceptible in the *Crucifixion,* is accentuated here, and the whole tragedy is expressed by Christ's posture. His body lies on His mother's lap, and His head, trunk, thighs, and calves form four different lines. Death dislocates His body by creating three breaks. The bodies depicted by Michelangelo are often articulated in a similarly artificial fashion which brings forth the deep meaning of the work. This is the reason why the *Pietà* may be called a masterpiece: In great works of art, the viewer is touched less by their theme than by the shaping and placement of the components which structure the work's space.

The Bruges *Madonna* is a hieratic figure (see p. 18). Christ Child is standing between her knees. Her back is straight, her eyes are cast down, and she seems to be meditating over the tragic fate which will befall her son. As the viewer becomes slowly aware of the play of forms in the sculpture, he may discover its intellectual tension, which is typical of all works by Michelangelo. The child's disjointed posture contrasts with his mother's stiffness. This diverging orientation of the two bodies is then enclosed in the sculpture's oval shape, which calls to mind medieval mandorlas marking a sacred presence. This work, however, was made at the same time as the *Madonna with Child* now in the collection of the Bargello Museum in Florence and the *David*. These three works have one trait in common: The oval outline of the Bruges *Madonna*, the round tondo, and the slimness of the *David* evoke the original shape of the stone blocks from which they were carved. Many sculptors, such as Bernini, applied their virtuosity to

Pietà, 1499. Marble, height 68 1/2" (174 cm)
Saint Peter's Basilica, Rome. Photo Scala, Florence

Madonna with Child (The Bruges Madonna), 1501? Marble, height 50 3/8" (128 cm)
Church of Notre-Dame, Bruges. Photo Institut Royal du Patrimoine Artistique, Brussels

hiding the constraints and resistance of the stone they worked. Michelangelo sought exactly the opposite effect. From his early works to the *Slaves* of the 1530s and the unfinished *Pietà Rondanini*, he showed that the sculptor carving marble was struggling with a stone which imposed its own constraints. It is known that Michelangelo wished and loved this confrontation between the sculptor and the hard stone. As an artist, he saw more clearly than others that his ideas could take shape only in the course of a sometimes violent dialogue in his own artistic idiom. He felt contempt for sculptors working in wax or clay. He used to say that they worked "per forza di porre," adding layer upon layer of matter, in a relationship with the work which was akin to a caress. He wanted to work "per forza di levare," chipping stone away from stone. Michelangelo was unfair toward other techniques of sculpture, but he expressed a major idea of artists of all times and all kinds: The artist coerces a shape out of matter which inspires in him an idiom. At first, this matter may be a shapeless block of marble, but it has its own constraints and it leads the hand and mind working on it.

The *Mother and Child* of the tondo Pitti features three figures: the Virgin Mary, Child Christ, and Saint John as a child (see p. 12). The three figures are slightly bent, following the round shape of the overall sculpture. *David* is an even more striking example of this passionate dialogue between Michelangelo and a block of stone (see pp. 20 and 21). This stone had a long history. It came from a quarry in Carrara and was first given to Agostino del Duccio to be carved into a gigantic face designed to decorate the façade of the cathedral. The work proved to be too difficult and was quickly abandoned. The stone remained untouched for almost forty years as no sculptor dared to carve it. The twenty-six-year old Michelangelo took up the challenge in 1500, when he returned to Florence. Here, the sculptor's awareness of the matter bore unusual results: The stone was a little narrow when used in its height to represent the correct proportions of a man's body. Michelangelo took the stone as it was. The figure of *David* took into account the characteristics imparted by chance. *David* was carved with a thinner body than he might have been otherwise, but Michelangelo gave him a posture both restrained and dynamic, and this internal tension makes the work monumental. The right-hand side of David's body forms a straight line: The arm is hanging almost loose; the straight leg carries the weight of the whole body. Contrasting with this double straight line, the other leg is stretched leftward and the left arm is bent. This play of forms creates a tension expressing the strength of character and the self-control of the biblical hero. Vasari reported that the Florentines viewed *David* as the representation of the values which should lead the new republic and they placed it on the Piazza della Signoria, where it became the symbol of the city.

Michelangelo returned to Rome in March 1505. Pope Julius II had called him to design his tomb, which was supposed to be a monumental work decorated with several statues. By 1506 Julius II changed his mind because he could not finance all of his projects. He gave priority to the construction of the new Saint Peter's Basilica, for

David, 1501-1504. Marble, height 172³/₈" (434 cm)
Accademia, Florence. Photo Nicolò Orsi Battaglini, Florence

David. Side view
Photo Nicolò Orsi Battaglini, Florence

A Seated Nude Man, undated
Pen, brown and grayish-brown ink
grayish-brown wash
heightened with white
16 ⁹/₁₆" × 11 ⁵/₁₆" (42.1 × 28.7 cm)
The British Museum, London
Gift of H. Vaughan

which he commissioned the painter and architect Donato Bramante (1444-1514). Michelangelo felt offended and humiliated because he was barred from the Vatican. He fled to Florence, without asking his leave, as he should have done. A few months later, the Pope took back the city of Bologna and Michelangelo went there for a reconciliation. He was then commissioned to paint the ceiling of the Sistine Chapel.

Michelangelo had already painted the *Madonna Doni* (see p. 5), now at the Uffizi Gallery in Florence. The work is interesting because of the choices he made. His figures — the Virgin Mary, Christ Child, Saint Joseph — have muscular bodies; they seem like giants, or at least athletes. They form a group in which arms, legs, and bodies are intertwined, their mass resembling a sculpture carved in a single stone. The bright, slightly sharp, colors highlight this sculptural effect. The figures evoke statues placed in the open. Michelangelo was clearly painting with sculpture in mind: He created carefully constructed spaces and his mingled bodies became independent blocks of space. In the background of the painting, nude male figures also evoke sculptures. Most importantly, Michelangelo did not use any chiaroscuro, neither for the composition of the central group nor for the relationship between the foreground and the distance. Leonardo da Vinci had pointed to the advantage of a systematic use of chiaroscuro. He believed it to be the most realistic means to reconcile linear and colored perspectives: In the same manner as parallel lines seem to join on the horizon, colors seem to turn gray at a far distance. Michelangelo preferred to use light tones and vary their luminosity. This solution found followers in the second half of the sixteenth century. It was too consistent a technique to be a choice Michelangelo would have made only to distinguish himself from Leonardo da Vinci, although the two men had somehow competed against one another. In 1504 the

government of Florence had commissioned Leonardo da Vinci for the decoration of the council hall. He started a work on the *Battle of Anghiari*, but he left it unfinished. At the same time, Michelangelo was commissioned for another fresco in the same council hall. He designed a picture of the *Battle of Cascina*, the studies of which are extant (see p. 23). Whatever the rivalry between the two artists, Michelangelo's preference for the play of colors to express depth of space was certainly as valid a choice as the use of chiaroscuro. While there are no decisive arguments in the matter, this observation about colors may apply when the recent restoration of the frescoes in the Sistine Chapel is questioned. A symphony of sharp colors replaced a deep chiaroscuro, the dark tones of which may have been due only to dirt accumulating for centuries on the ceiling. These sharp colors were favored by the so-called Mannerist painters, who painted in the manner of the artists of the high Renaissance, and Michelangelo in particular. Michelangelo may have chosen this very bright range of colors because he disagreed with the fashion for chiaroscuro. The restoration, however, may also have scraped more than accumulated dirt, it may have removed a varnish which Michelangelo possibly applied himself to soften the brightness of his colors.

He worked for four years, from 1508 to 1512, on the frescoes of the ceiling in the Sistine Chapel. It must have been a painful task. He would have preferred working on the tomb of Julius II, for which his preparatory studies were very advanced. This would have been a sculptor's work, something more familiar than this huge endeavor as a painter. Michelangelo never painted pictures. All his paintings, with the exception of the *Madonna Doni*, were meant to decorate an architectural work. Moreover, the decoration of the Sistine Chapel required a very stern discipline. The work had to be done on a very high scaffolding, from which he could rarely come down to go back up. Therefore, they were four years spent in great solitude. It must have been also a period of great mental stress. His accomplishment was unique: He conceived and achieved an immense decor, painted on a vault, the curving of which must have made it very difficult to place the figures in a perspective view. This was an astonishing achievement. He displayed the greatest mastery as he integrated a visual decor in an architectural construction, with figures merging symbolically with architectural components. And the representational imagination of the artist reached the highest level. In the beginning, frescoes decorated the lower portion of walls in the Sistine Chapel. Several fifteenth-century artists had painted the story of Moses on the wall on the left, and the story of Christ on the wall on the right. Thus, pictures from the Old and the New Testaments were facing one another. On the space given to him, which was much vaster, Michelangelo chose to illustrate the Creation itself, this event outside of time, which preceded the historic time of the Hebrews and the Christians.

Before the viewer proceeds to "read" the stories as they unfold on the successive parts of the vault, his imagination is struck by the space of the paintings, more precisely by their concept of space. In the Sistine Chapel Michelangelo reached out to the symbolic unity between man's labor as he builds his home on earth and the imaginary space which nourishes his mind. The whole space becomes both a stage for actions by which men are brought together and tied to the soil, and an opportunity to dream and create figures which express the artist's beliefs. This effort to keep together the results of both the technical work and thoughts of man is the highest expression of humanist philosophy. One must be struck by this spectacular reversal of the concept of space from earlier times. In the Middle Ages and the early Renaissance, the paintings decorating princely and religious buildings, palaces, and churches developed an imaginary world which was independent of the architectural structure. One could even say that they were meant to hide this structure, which evoked the physical process of building, while the paintings were meant to bring spiritual truth to the fore. The world of man's actions was then separate from that of revealed religious truth, and the realm of

Bacchus Drunk, 1496-1497. Marble, height 79 $^{15}/_{16}$" (203 cm)
Bargello, Florence. Photo Nicolò Orsi Battaglini, Florence

the divine from that of man. Michelangelo's approach was as bold as that of Giordano Bruno (1548-1600), who was burnt at the stake for putting it into words. Michelangelo conceived of the sacred as a result of man's labor as he struggles with the physical reality of the world and builds houses, palaces, and temples. While Pope Julius II had an ambitious idea when he decided that the long vault of the Sistine Chapel be decorated with significant episodes from the Christian religion, Michelangelo proved to be even more ambitious. After a few preparatory designs, he asked that the decoration extend below to the lunettes and the triangles supporting the vault. This extension of the surface to be painted was significant: The placement of the pictures must be part of the organization of the sacred space, and this space must have both an architectural and a symbolic value, which cannot be separated from one another.

Looking up to the ceiling of the Sistine Chapel, the viewer is immediately struck by the fact that Michelangelo enhanced the structure of the vault by painting fake architectural components: A string-course, pilasters, cornices, which were added to the triangles and lunettes outlined by the construction. These architectural components — some real, some imitated in painting — create a complicated squaring of the vault. The length of the center part is divided into nine panels. Starting from the chancel and moving toward the entrance door, Michelangelo featured scenes of the Creation on each panel and a few scenes from the life of mankind shortly after the Fall. This series of pictures makes a story: The artist chose the high points of a history, the continuity of which is easy to reconstruct. And this continuity lies in the meaning to man's existence in a universe created by God, as given by the Bible and the Christian religion (see p. 27).

The meaning of man's adventure is not expressed only by this historic continuity. In its width, the vault is divided into three orders: The center is the setting for the story of the Creation; below — and separated from the center by a string-course — comes a series of gigantic figures, Sibyls from ancient Greek civilization and Prophets from the Bible (see pp. 28, 29, 30, 31, and 33). The Sibyls were the prophets of pagan times, while the Prophets announce God's words. On the architectural triangles and the lunettes, Michelangelo depicted scenes from the Bible and the trials of different prominent characters who preceded Christ (see pp. 43, 44, and 45). As the three orders are viewed from the bottom up, they mark a progression, from the description of the daily life of figures similar to us to the evocation of prophets who receive God's words — in a more obscure fashion for the ancient Sibyls, more clearly for the Biblical Prophets. The viewer's mind is drawn into a rising motion culminating in the scenes from the Creation, where the ultimate meaning of things is revealed. The power of Michelangelo's mind is nothing less but astonishing, as his ability to formulate the details and consistency of a highly complex philosophy. He presented a whole cosmology in terms of the Christian religion, the history of our earth and of mankind. Of course, the components of this philosophy are drawn from traditional Christian teachings; they are

THE VAULT OF THE SISTINE CHAPEL. General view, 1506 (?)-1512
Fresco. Photo Musei del Vaticano

THE DELPHIC SIBYL, detail, 1509. Fresco
Musei del Vaticano, Sistine Chapel, The Vault. Photo P. Zigrossi

DELPHICA

THE DELPHIC SIBYL, 1509. Fresco, 137³/₄" × 149⁵/₈" (350 × 380 cm)
Musei del Vaticano, Sistine Chapel, The Vault. Photo P. Zigrossi

THE PROPHET DANIEL, 1511. Fresco, 155 1/2" × 149 5/8" (395 × 380 cm)
Musei del Vaticano, Sistine Chapel, The Vault. Photo P. Zigrossi

THE CUMAEAN SIBYL, 1510. Fresco, 147 ⁵/₈" × 149 ⁵/₈" (375 × 380 cm)
Musei del Vaticano, Sistine Chapel, The Vault. Photo P. Zigrossi

ESAIAS

NUDE FIGURE NEXT TO THE SCENE OF NOAH'S
SACRIFICE, detail, 1509. Fresco
Musei del Vaticano, Sistine Chapel, The Vault
Photo P. Zigrossi

THE PROPHET ISAIAH, 1509
Fresco, 143 ⁵/₈" × 149 ⁵/₈" (365 × 380 cm)
Musei del Vaticano, Sistine Chapel, The Vault
Photo P. Zigrossi

33

not invented.   The novelty, however, lies in the order and relationship in which they are presented.   This essential novelty is in the connection between the architectural work of man and the symbolism which gives it a meaning.

The trompe-l'œil structure which Michelangelo added when painting the ceiling of the Sistine Chapel bring to light a fundamental humanist idea, which remains valid to this day: Man gives a meaning to the world by creating an order in the physical space of this world, to the point where he rises to the idea of God.   The cornices of the painted pilasters feature naked adolescent boys, *ignudi* (see p. 32).   Their posture indicates that these cornices are symbols of the cohesive architectural forces by which the retaining walls prevent the massive vault from collapsing.   By contrast, the sheer size of the gigantic Sibyls and Prophets increases the impression that the whole construction weighs massively on the ground, that is it is rooted in the earth.   Therefore, Michelangelo did more than depict the historic meaning given to mankind by the Christian culture: He also expressed one of the deepest humanist ideas most convincingly. The paintings in the Sistine Chapel are a strong statement that the meaning of things is always the result of man's work as he struggles with the physical world and creates the necessary buildings and tools.   This very general idea is then applied to the uniqueness of the artist's work.   As Michelangelo created a symbolic order on the surface of the ceiling in the Sistine Chapel, he claimed that the social function of the artist — the painter, the sculptor, and the architect — is to impart a full meaning to the placement of the elements of man's space.

As the viewer enters the Sistine Chapel through the great door in the back and walks toward the altar, he looks up and reads the story of a time before that of the Hebrews, the Bible and the Gospel, when man was grieving the loss of paradise.   Michelangelo evoked the story of Noah, his drunkenness, his sacrifice, the Flood (see p. 35), and the Ark by which God gave another chance to the world he had created.   As the viewer walks toward the altar, he proceeds from this time of desolation to early events caused by man's deeds and his original sin.   First, he sees Adam and Eve driven out of the garden of Eden, the apple picked, the snake coiling around the tree, the Angel's terrifying gesture, Adam and Eve in tears (see p. 36).   Clearly Michelangelo was leading the viewer along a path toward initiation.   Starting from a statement about mankind's permanent unhappiness after it betrayed God's trust, the viewer progresses step by step toward the mystery of Creation itself, toward God's will that mankind be free.   There is *The Creation of Eve*, then *The Creation of Adam*, which stands as the strongest statement ever of the relationship between man and his Maker (see pp. 38-39).   The fingers of God and Adam reach toward one another but they fail to touch.   This is the most intense expression of man's tragic fate.   And this intensity finds an echo in the striking deeds of *God Separating the Water from the Earth*, *God Creating the Moon and the Sun*, and *God Separating the Light from the Shadows* (see pp. 42, 41, and 40).

THE FLOOD
Detail of the left side, 1508-1509
Fresco
Musei del Vaticano, Sistine Chapel, The Vault
Photo P. Zigrossi

THE ORIGINAL SIN (ADAM AND EVE DRIVEN OUT OF THE GARDEN OF EDEN), detail, 1509-1510. Fresco
Musei del Vaticano, Sistine Chapel, The Vault. Photo P. Zigrossi

The latter picture may be seen as a symbol of Michelangelo's artistic endeavor during the four years he dedicated to the ceiling of the Sistine Chapel. *The Creation of Adam* depicts both man's desire to unite with God and the obvious distance between them; it marks a particularly dramatic moment. The separation of the light from the shadows, however, is a picture which leads the mind even further. It suggests a meditation on man's own intellectual work and, above all, the significance which the artist's work must have. All the preceding scenes feature several figures, each scene depicting the details of a different and complex story. The picture of *God Separating the Light from the Shadows* features only the Maker. It evokes a simple event: Where there had been only chaos, suddenly there was something. Light emerged from the shadows. The origins of everything, and the origin of thought, lies in this duality by which the mind can conceive of one thing as the opposite of another. This distinction between day and night, and all other distinction in terms of opposites, are only possible

Study of a Reclining Male Nude, undated
This drawing may be a study for
The Creation of Adam
Red chalk, 7 9/16" × 10 1/4" (19.3 × 25.9 cm)
The British Museum, London

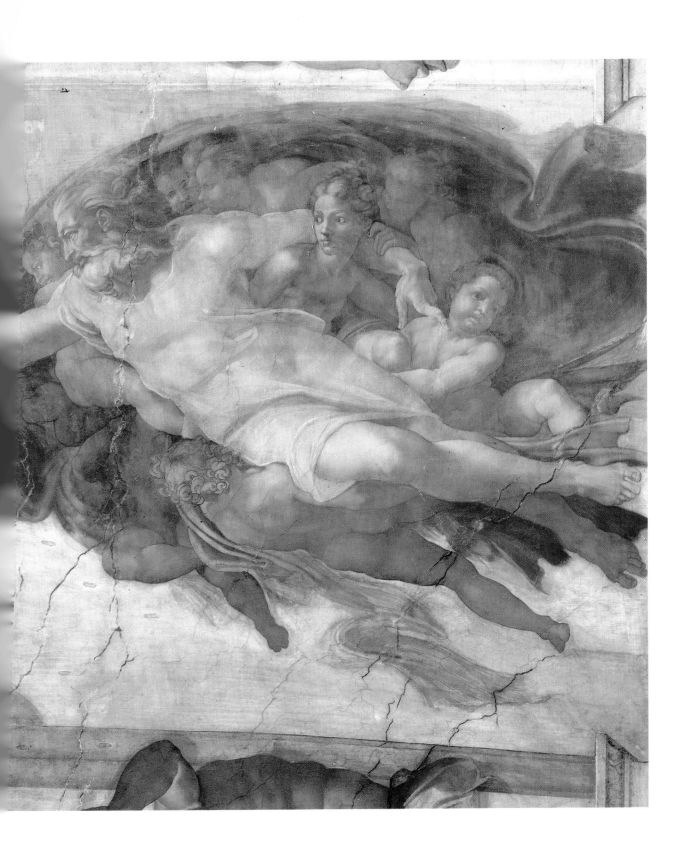

THE CREATION OF ADAM, 1510
Fresco, 110 $^{1}/_{4}$" × 98 $^{3}/_{8}$" (280 × 250 cm)
Musei del Vaticano, Sistine Chapel, The Vault
Photo P. Zigrossi

God Separating the Light from the Shadows
Detail, 1510
Fresco
Musei del Vaticano, Sistine Chapel, The Vault
Photo P. Zigrossi

THE CREATION OF HEAVENLY BODIES
GOD CREATING THE MOON AND THE SUN, detail, 1510
Fresco
Musei del Vaticano, Sistine Chapel, The Vault
Photo P. Zigrossi

41

A Lunette: Jacob and Joseph, 1511-1512
Fresco after restoration
84 5/8" × 169 1/4" (215 × 430 cm)
Musei del Vaticano, Sistine Chapel, The Vault
Photo P. Zigrossi

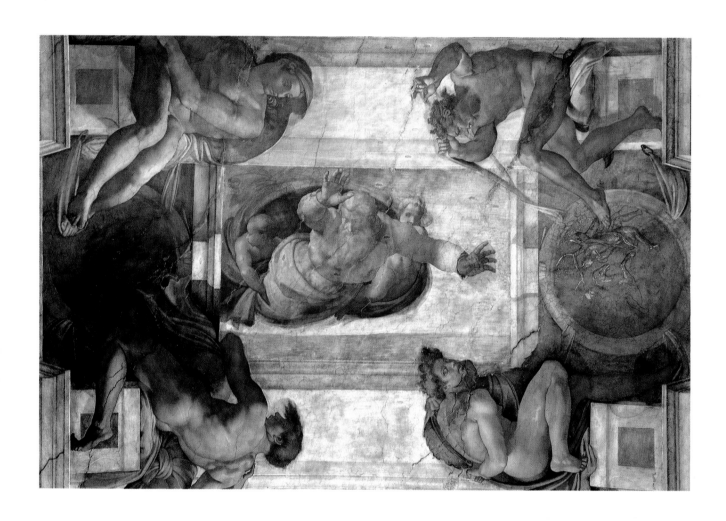

God Separating the Water from the Earth
and Ignudi, 1511
Fresco, 61" × 106 1/4" (155 × 270 cm)
Musei del Vaticano, Sistine Chapel, The Vault
Photo P. Zigrossi

A Lunette: Asa, Josephat and Joram, 1511-1512
Fresco after restoration
84 5/8" × 169 1/4" (215 × 430 cm)
Musei del Vaticano, Sistine Chapel, The Vault
Photo P. Zigrossi

A Lunette: Nason, detail of the left side, 1511-1512. Fresco after restoration
Musei del Vaticano, Sistine Chapel, The Vault. Photo P. Zigrossi

A Lunette: Aminadab, detail of the right side, 1511-1512. Fresco after restoration
Musei del Vaticano, Sistine Chapel, The Vault. Photo P. Zigrossi

because the mind is set in motion.   Mind and matter are one, the former giving life to the latter, and man can conceive of all the realities of the world because of this dynamic process.   This is where the divine lies: The Biblical picture of God presented by Michelangelo is a whirling shape, whose own circular motion and the ones it provokes are a symbol of the mind in action.   Michelangelo conceived of the world's beauty as entirely created by the strength, one might say the violence, of this motion uniting man's mind with the world's body.   This is the other name of God.

After Michelangelo finished the Sistine Chapel, he wished to take up the work that was the most important to him, the monumental tomb for Julius II, where he could express fully his mastery of his art as a sculptor.   The Pope died in 1513, however.   Michelangelo signed a contract with the Pope's heirs and resumed work on the mausoleum.   He carved *The Rebellious Slave*, *The Dying Slave* (see pp. 47 and 49), and *Moses* (see p. 77), sculptures which were all intended for the monument.   But the new Pope, Leon X, wished to send Michelangelo away from Rome.   He ordered him to design and build the San Lorenzo Church in Florence.   Thus Michelangelo returned to his native city.   Once again, the Pope had been too ambitious and he could not finance the very expensive construction of the façade.   Consequently, Michelangelo was faced with many difficulties.   He did not stop, however, and resumed work on the tomb of Julius II, but the construction was again interrupted by the heirs of the late Pope.

In 1520, Michelangelo was commissioned to do a more modest work, which he could bring to a satisfactory, albeit not ideal, stage.   He agreed to take over the design and interior decoration of the Medici Chapel, inside the San Lorenzo Church (see pp. 52 and 53).   The Pope had decided that this chapel was to be turned into a memorial chapel containing the tombs of Lorenzo and Giuliano de Medici.   The tombs of two other members of the family, Lorenzo, Duke of Urbino, and Giuliano, Duke of Nemours, were also to be placed in the chapel.   Just as the other important works had been overly ambitious, this one could not be as grand as its patrons — and Michelangelo — had first hoped.   The chapel became a memorial to the two "great" Medici only, Lorenzo and Giuliano, and Michelangelo gave up the idea of a construction in the center.   The two tombs are placed on opposite walls, facing one another.   The other two walls feature the altar and a sculpture of the *Madonna with Child* (see p. 51).   Nevertheless, the chapel stands as one of Michelangelo's masterpieces.   Like the ceiling of the Sistine Chapel, it achieves a remarkable integration of the architecture, the paintings, and the sculptures. This intentional integration of the figures, and its symbolic meaning, is even more visible than in the Sistine Chapel.   The architecture of the chapel is structured by columns, pilasters, and different arches; the tombs are structured in a similar fashion, so that they are closely connected to the whole building.   The statues of Lorenzo and Giuliano are placed above the tombs.   Two nude statues, one a man, the other a woman, lie on each of the sarcophagi.   On Lorenzo's tomb, the male nude is a symbol of *Twilight* (see p. 54); the female nude is *Dawn* (see p. 55).   On Giuliano's tomb, *Day* is a male nude (see p. 56),

The Rebellious Slave, 1513. Marble for the tomb of Julius II, unfinished. Height 84 ⁵/₈" (215 cm)
Musée du Louvre, Paris. Photo Réunion des Musées Nationaux, Paris

Saint Matthew, ca 1504. Preliminary carving for the Duomo in Florence, height 102 ³/₄" (261 cm)
Accademia, Florence. Photo Nicolò Orsi Battaglini, Florence

The Dying Slave, 1513. Marble for the second version of the tomb of Julius II Height 90 ¹/₈" (229 cm). Musée du Louvre, Paris. Photo Réunion des Musées Nationaux, Paris

while *Night* is a woman.   Thus death is inscribed in three time dimensions.   The time suggested by the nude figures is a cycle, by which night is followed by day, and twilight by dawn.   The figures of Lorenzo and Giuliano wear ancient armor, evoking the culture of ancient Greece and Rome and a historic time.   Finally, the Madonna with Child stands for that which is outside of time, an eternity which is God's privilege.   Michelangelo's meditation about death brings the viewer to a disconcerting reflection on the plurality of time which, in turn, is characteristic of a spatial plurality.   Man's space has also different dimensions, referring to the divine, the cosmic, the terrestrial, and the everyday life.   The artist's task is the same in all cultures: Together, the painter, the sculptor, and the architect propose to measure the space in which man lives; they mark it out, and give it a symbolic meaning as they define it.   The meaning of the Medici Chapel reaches out to the essence of things: The tombs evoke death; the Virgin nursing her Child evokes life.   These symbols refer also to a hierarchy: The divine, the cosmic, and the human are orders of space and time which are defined in every culture.   The humanism of the Renaissance, as it was viewed by Michelangelo, places man at the crossing of these different dimensions in time and space.

Humanism defined man as the gauge of everything.   In the same manner, the painter and the sculptor took man's vision as the gauge for everything visible in the world.   The perspective representation of space is based on man's point of view.   Nothing can be seen but from this point of view.   In a very consistent fashion, humanist philosophers invoked man's universal rationality when making a judgment on truth, and they referred all judgment on taste to a system of rules which they believed to have come from the rationality of ancient Greece and Rome.   These principles of rationalist humanism were to lead to the scientific knowledge based on rationality.   Similarly, they were at the source of the art which was called "classic" because it appeared to be the rational conclusion of all artistic thoughts.   These ideas, no doubt, became too rigid at times and developed into so-called "academic art." It makes it even more moving to see how Michelangelo's approach excludes all simplification and rigidity, how rich and complex it is.   It evokes the multiple dimensions of time and space, while it keeps the human mind at the center of all understanding, and the body as the symbol and the cornerstone of man's concept of space.   All his ideas about the human body — the swaying hips of the *Christ* carved in wood, the posture of *David* and the gigantic figures in the Sistine Chapel — refer to the same principles: The body, its head, trunk, arms, and legs, is articulated in several intersecting lines.   Let us contemplate the *Night* in the Medici Chapel (see p. 57): The head and its heavy braid, the right arm, the chest, the stomach, the left thigh, each creates a line which divides the space with a different orientation.   Its body is like a three-dimensional compass card, like a sextant which helps to find stars and leads to dreams about the infinite space of the cosmos.   *The Night* is a very moving image: A human body bearing the future marks of oncoming age evokes the death which is in every man, and it creates a connection with the cosmos.   It orients the viewer, making him recognize the conditions of his life and death, making him think about his fate.

Madonna with Child, 1521-1531. Marble, height 88 ¹⁵/₁₆" (226 cm)
San Lorenzo, Florence. Photo Nicolò Orsi Battaglini, Florence

Study for a Double Tomb:
Figure for a Sarcophagus, 1516-1532
Black chalk, 10³/₈" × 7 ⁷/₁₆" (26.4 × 18.8 cm)
The British Museum, London

Tomb of Giuliano de Medici, 1526-1533
General view
Medici Chapel, San Lorenzo, Florence
Photo Nicolò Orsi Battaglini, Florence

Twilight. Allegorical Figure
1524-1531
Marble, tomb of Lorenzo de Medici
Length 76 ³/₄" (195 cm)
Medici Chapel, San Lorenzo, Florence
Photo Nicolò Orsi Battaglini, Florence

Dawn. Allegorical Figure
1524-1531
Marble, tomb of Lorenzo de Medici
Length 80" (203 cm)
Medici Chapel, San Lorenzo, Florence
Photo Nicolò Orsi Battaglini, Florence

Day. Allegorical Figure
1526-1533
Marble, tomb of Giuliano de Medici
Length 71 7/8" (185 cm)
Medici Chapel, San Lorenzo, Florence
Photo Nicolò Orsi Battaglini, Florence

Night. Allegorical Figure
1526-1533
Marble, tomb of Giuliano de Medici
Medici Chapel, San Lorenzo, Florence
Photo Nicolò Orsi Battaglini, Florence

Another troubled and adventurous period started for Michelangelo, but it was to be brief. It revealed another trait of his personality, namely his political support for the republican regime which Florence attempted to establish. Later, when he was firmly settled in Rome, he expressed similar liberal views. He became close to the religious society of the Oratory of Divine Love and several figures around the religious reformer Juan de Valdés. He was, above all, a man who loved freedom. He belonged to the group of humanists who wished for a more egalitarian society and were opposed to the narrowmindedness of the Counter-Reformation. In 1527, Rome was pillaged. In Florence, the Medici were overthrown for a second time and replaced by a republic which lasted only three years. The Pope and the Spanish emperor Charles V were about to besiege the city. Michelangelo offered to work on the fortifications and was put in charge of their improvement. He drew several designs, which are extant. He may have been suddenly frightened, for he fled to Ferrara and continued to Venice. It is said that he intended to take refuge in France. Then he returned to Florence just as suddenly. The siege had just started and he worked again on the fortifications. When Florence fell, he went into hiding in order to avoid imprisonment, but Pope Clement VII was too aware of Michelangelo's talent as an artist not to forgive him. Michelangelo was able to finish his work on the Medici Chapel and he made sculptures for his new patrons. In 1534, he settled in Rome. He had recently met Tommaso Cavalieri, a young Roman patrician of great beauty, who was also a very educated man. Cavalieri had a good knowledge of ancient literature and he collected art works from ancient Rome. He was quite typical of the circles that nurtured the Neo-Platonic philosophy which left its imprint on the whole Italian Renaissance. Michelangelo was steeped in the same classic writers. In his youth he had known such humanists as Marsile Ficino at the court of Lorenzo de Medici. He was also brought up on the models of statues from ancient Greece and Rome. A few letters from the correspondence of the two men are extant, as well as many poems by Michelangelo, the original text of which was established in the nineteenth century. There are several love poems dedicated to Tommaso Cavalieri. As Michelangelo was growing older and becoming close to Vittoria Colonna and the society of the Oratory of Divine Love, his poems expressed the rise of man's love to the love of God. This would confirm the opinion that Michelangelo was influenced by Neo-Platonic philosophy. His love affair with Cavalieri and the poems dedicated to him would show that he sublimated his carnal desire in a desire for the mystical fusion of their souls.

The search for the influence of philosophical doctrines on Michelangelo's work may lead to a neglect of the artist's ideas and intentions. This happens often because it is easy to reduce everything to a few abstract ideas. The humanists of the Renaissance read and meditated over the writings by Plato, no doubt, and Michelangelo must have been steeped in this culture. His own contribution to humanism, however, owes nothing to Plato or any other philosopher. This is made evident by both his poems and his work as a sculptor and painter. His paintings and sculptures create a space which is not

Portrait of Andrea Quaratesi, 1520-1532
Black chalk, $16^{3}/_{8}$" × $11^{1}/_{2}$" (41.1 × 29.2 cm). The British Museum, London. Malcolm Collection

Female Half-length Figure, undated
Black chalk
12 ¹¹/₁₆" × 10 ¹/₈" (32.3 × 25.8 cm)
The British Museum, London

solely defined by the static point of view of perspective. Michelangelo did not regard the body as an eye that keeps still. This body belongs entirely to the space of the earth and the cosmos. This is a body open to the outside, whose imagination projects itself to give shape to that outside world. As for Michelangelo's poetry, it is not sure that its idealized feeling of love refers to Platonic philosophy. He lived in a circle which was also influenced by a much more recent tradition, the strength of which was so great that, to this day, it continues to influence the arts. This tradition was that of Petrarch (1304-1374), Dante Alighieri (1265-1321), and, earlier still, that of the Italian poets of *dolce stil novo*, which was close to the troubadours in *Langue d'Oc*. According to this tradition, the feeling of love derives from the work the poet does with words to write the poems dedicated to his beloved. The artist's situation is quite similar: Spaces are created by erecting buildings and decorating them with symbolic figures. This concept of the artist's work and its effects on the mind was essential to the philosophy of Renaissance artists. It was entirely "modern," and it remains so to this day. Indeed, our modern world finds its economic and political roots in the life of fourteenth-century Italian cities. Humanist rationality, from which science was to be born, was part of this development. At the same time, all the arts were growing progressively apart from religion and politics. Their task in this modern context was to maintain the sharpness of the emotional bond between man and the physical reality he knows. This was indeed the tangible relationship between man and the world which Michelangelo conceived as a combination of the body and its different spatial dimensions. This was also the relationship the troubadours called "fin amors." So-called "modern love" was invented at the same time and by the same people who invented art as "art," as ideas separate from religion and politics. Michelangelo was the first painter or sculptor who was also a poet. His dual work, made of love poems and a new approach to space, can be viewed as that of an artist-philosopher. His poems as well as his statues expressed a new concept of life and destiny, which entailed a dynamic and passionate relationship between the world's sensitive and physical realities.

Ideal Head of a Woman, ca 1525-1528. Black chalk, 11 $\frac{1}{4}$" × 9 $\frac{1}{4}$" (28.7 × 23.5 cm)
The British Museum, London. Malcolm Collection

THE LAST JUDGMENT, detail
CHRIST, 1537-1541
Fresco
Musei del Vaticano, Sistine Chapel
Photo P. Zigrossi

THE LAST JUDGMENT
General view, 1537-1541
Fresco, 44'11 1/2" × 40' 3/8" (1370 × 1220 cm)
Musei del Vaticano, Sistine Chapel
Photo P. Zigrossi

63

Michelangelo settled in Rome in 1534. He did not leave it again, except for a brief escapade, and he died there in 1564. By then he had become the Pope's favorite artist. Clement VII commissioned him for a fresco on the wall at the back of the Sistine Chapel. Michelangelo painted the *Last Judgment*, which broke with the traditional rendering of this theme (see p. 65). Instead of a spatial hierarchy by which the damned are rejected to the bottom of the picture and the elected are elevated to the sky, Michelangelo created an aerial space which could be described as a whirl. Christ raises His arm in a vengeful manner and seems to stand at the center of a cyclone. Cloudy masses separated by empty space seem to carry groups of naked figures in a spiraling motion around Him. It is not easy to detect which bodies are on their way to heaven, and which are sent to hell. They all seem to be twisted by an inner violence, and they all resist this violence in an effort which tightens their athletic muscles. The scene is the more violent because it depicts the resurrection of the dead as well as the Last Judgment. The bodies are starting to tear themselves from the earth as they break through its crust. Some are still half interred, while others are covered with the mud out of which they are barely emerging. Michelangelo staged man as the tragic victim of an overwhelming fate against which he pits all his strength. As a result, the representation of the bodies is perfectly attuned to that of the space around them: They are twisted by the same motion. Christ seems a vengeful God, He is the one who, according to the Gospel, has come to bring war and not peace. In the middle of all this violence, pity is represented by the Mother of Christ, whose body appears to recoil as if she wanted to be out of the storm's reach. There is also some pity expressed by the wretched, as a man helps another and supports him in his anguish.

Michelangelo's humanism was not soft. After *The Last Judgment*, the two frescoes he painted in the Pauline Chapel are also marked by violence: *The Conversion of Saint Paul* (see page 69) and *The Crucifixion of Saint Peter* (see page 67), in a style close to that of *The Last Judgment*. The characteristic and meaning of *The Last Judgment* were amplified by the vastness of the painted surface. Michelangelo pointed to grief and death, to the hard desire to survive which leads men to struggle against the physical world. He also emphasized the courage of mankind. The figures which can be recognized as that of the damned are not presented as the traditional powerless victims of the torture inflicted by the Devil. They struggle, they resist, they rebel as they are dragged toward Hell. Michelangelo was sixty-five years old by then. He may have been obsessed by death, but he confronted this idea and fought against fear. A younger viewer, however, would not fail to be struck by this work, although he may not be yet preoccupied with death. He would be struck by the stormy motion in the work and its meanings. The whirling space in Michelangelo's *The Last Judgment* stands as a metaphor for the infinite cosmic space carrying away mankind, which feels it is the victim of entirely overwhelming forces. To this day, the image of whirling shapes serves as a representation of interstellar space. Michelangelo did not know the work of Copernicus, nor did Copernicus know Michelangelo's. But

Lamentation over the Dead Christ
1530-1535
Black chalk, partly stippled
11 1/8" × 10 5/16" (28.2 × 26.2 cm)
The British Museum, London

THE LAST JUDGMENT, detail, 1537-1541
SAINT BARTHOLOMEW
Fresco
Musei del Vaticano, Sistine Chapel
Photo P. Zigrossi

THE CRUCIFIXION OF SAINT PETER, detail
1545-1550
Fresco
Musei del Vaticano, Pauline Chapel
Photo T. Okamura

they must have had a kindred imagination since one proposed a new formula of gravitational astronomy centered on the sun, and the other, a view of man's body as if it were carried away by the stormy winds of fate. Michelangelo seems to illustrate the meditation formulated a century later by the philosopher Blaise Pascal, for whom man within nature was nothing compared to infinity, everything compared to nothingness, and something between nothing and everything. But unlike Pascal, who declared to be frightened by the silence of infinite space, Michelangelo seemed to be aware of only the sound and the fury.

During his last years in Rome, Michelangelo achieved unequaled fame. The artists who could have remained his rivals — Leonardo da Vinci, Raphael — were dead. The younger generation did not bring forth any character of similar stature. The young artists who admired and revered Michelangelo were called "Mannerists," because their art consisted of formal variations in the manner of their elder. They only kept the sort of graceful posture in Michelangelo's figures, the swaying hips by which the bodies create a spiral motion.

The figures in *The Last Judgment* are tormented bodies, but they are also powerfully built and violent. By contrast, some of Michelangelo's late sculptures have graceful shapes, long and supple — as in *Victory*, which was meant for the tomb of Julius II, and even *The Pietà Rondanini*, a work which Michelangelo could not finish before he died, and where the mother holding her dead son seems to tear herself and him from the earth. This latter work comes at the end of Michelangelo's long evolution as a sculptor. His first preliminary studies for the tomb of Julius II dated back to 1505, and Michelangelo devoted exactly forty years to this work. The design of the tomb has a long, complicated history. As it now stands at San Pietro in Vincoli, it is the result of many designs which were progressively pared down, mostly for financial reasons. This evolution was also due to the rivalry between Bramante and Michelangelo regarding the design of Saint Peter's Basilica and the clashes between Michelangelo and the heirs to the Pope. These changes were punctuated by a series of statues which are a magnificent expression of Michelangelo's mature art.

Michelangelo's different designs for the tomb of Julius II show that he planned a monumental mausoleum, a building several story high, decorated with statues and placed at the center of Saint Peter's Basilica, the construction of which was about to be started. Julius II, however, chose to commission Bramante for the renovation of the basilica. Bramante adopted Michelangelo's proposal of a building with a central plan, but he intended to place at the center a commemorative chapel to Saint Peter's martyrdom. This solution excluded that Michelangelo's projected work be placed there. He felt deeply offended and, on August 17, 1506, on the eve of the breaking of the ground for the basilica, he fled to Florence. He only came back the following November, after he had met the pope in Bologna for a reconciliation. Throughout its

THE CONVERSION OF SAINT PAUL, detail, 1542-1545. Fresco
Musei del Vaticano, Pauline Chapel. Photo T. Okamura

different stages, Michelangelo's design for the tomb of Julius II was shaped like a triumphal arch, to celebrate the victory of the Roman Church at a time when Protestant movements were demanding a "Reformation" of the church and the Pope responded to these attacks by launching a "Counter-Reformation" and later creating the "Inquisition." Clearly, Michelangelo belonged to an open-minded and tolerant group that formed the backbone of the humanist movement. He could not view the triumph of the Roman Church as a moral defeat inflicted on a philosophical movement based on the "pagan" tradition of ancient Greece and Rome. The architectural structure of the tomb of Julius II found its inspiration in the pagan tradition of Rome's triumphal arches. The sculptures he created to give the work a clearly explicit meaning — such as *Moses* and the series of *Slaves* — were drawn from both the Bible and ancient Greece and Rome. Michelangelo belonged to a group of intellectuals who refused to set off Christian and pagan traditions against each other. His composition for the *Statue of Victory* seems to symbolize the victory of intelligence over fallacy rather than that of one culture over another. According to Michelangelo's humanist philosophy, truth cannot be viewed as the privilege of a period or a doctrine. It is a progressive conquest, to which all civilizations contribute in the course of history. His genius did not limit itself to adopting such general ideas about a struggle for truth as the basis for the community of man. As an artist, he did not think abstractly. His philosophy was expressed by this choice of figures drawn both from the Bible and ancient Greece and Rome, but also more concretely by a number of formal characteristics which capture the attention and the eye of the viewer.

The first characteristic is a consequence of Michelangelo's passionate love for working in stone. He felt that carving stone alone fulfills the sculptor's task, when he tears a shape from the shapeless, with the sole help of his chisel. This was seen as a significant symbol of man's labor, by which he struggles against matter in order to conquest his freedom. Already when Michelangelo was an adolescent, he showed this love for the hand-to-hand struggle with stone. This is particularly apparent in the bas-relief of *The Centaurs*, the theme of which is the trials and confrontation of men as they tear themselves from a chaotic battle and win their right to exist. The same drama is to be found in Michelangelo's paintings, especially in the scenes of resurrection in *The Last Judgment*. Among the works designed for the tomb of Julius II, the series of *The Slaves* is extant (see pp. 47, 49, and 71-74). These figures present a poignant rendering of mankind's dramatic fate. The slave is a man whom other men try to reduce to the status of an animal. He is bound to the land he tills just as animals and plants are bound to the land. He was born on this piece of land and this is where he will die. Our history, however, has seen countless rebellions of slaves. When Michelangelo carved his *Slaves*, he emphasized their rebellion and their will to tear themselves from their animal status and the constraints of solely physical work. This is made evident by a trait shared by all figures: The human shapes are still partly caught in the rough stone. The two first figures he carved, *The Rebellious Slave* and *The Dying Slave*, are

Slave (or Prisoner) called Atlas, 1519-1536. Preparatory marble for the tomb of Julius II Height 81⁷/₈" (208 cm). Accademia, Florence. Photo Nicolò Orsi Battaglini, Florence

*Slave (or Prisoner) Awaking, 1519-1536. Preparatory marble for the tomb of Julius II
Height 105" (267 cm). Accademia, Florence. Photo Nicolò Orsi Battaglini, Florence*

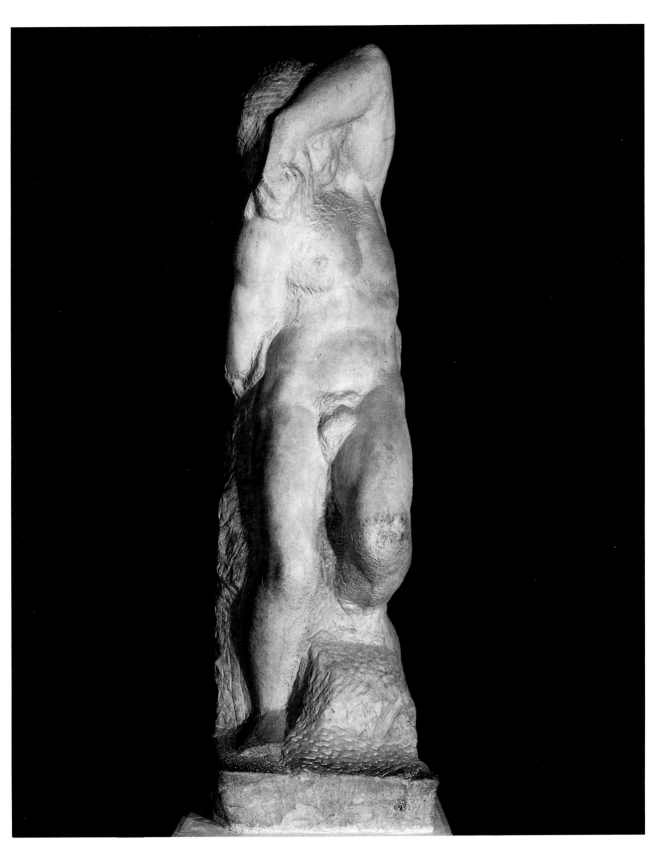

Young Slave (or Prisoner), 1519-1536. Preparatory marble for the tomb of Julius II Height 92 ¹/₂" (235 cm). Accademia, Florence. Photo Nicolò Orsi Battaglini, Florence

Bearded Slave (or Prisoner), 1519-1536. Preparatory marble for the tomb of Julius II
Height 97 ⁵/₈" (248 cm). Accademia, Florence. Photo Nicolò Orsi Battaglini, Florence

almost free from the stone (see pp. 47 and 49). The others are still one with the massive marble, from which they seem to rise through a terrible effort. It is true that the latter works are unfinished — *Atlas* and *The Slave Awaking* in particular (see pp. 71 and 72). But the very fact that they were left unfinished is also significant. Michelangelo worked for forty years on the tomb of Julius II, and his assistants could have chiseled the outlined shapes free from the stone. Michelangelo was mostly interested in the dynamic process of his own mind as he worked on this monument. He marked it with sculptures which were only carved outlines. Above all, he viewed his sculpture as an expression of this creative effort, of the sculptor's ability as a man to create. His work is to conquer that which is subjected to an overwhelming necessity. These unfinished statues stand as the highest expression of Michelangelo's ideas, as they reflect first of all a creative process and present a sculpture as a genesis.

The *Statue of Victory*, which is now in the Palazzo della Signoria in Florence, is one of the most finished works designed for the tomb of Julius II. The same can be said of *Moses*, which is placed at the center of the lower part of the tomb, as it now stands at the church of San Pietro in Vincoli. The same can be said also of *Lea* and *Rachel* on either side of *Moses*. They are finished because they were chosen for the final design of the tomb. *Victory* and *Moses* are the most remarkable. These two figures share certain traits, which are quite different from those characteristic of the *Slaves*, but significant no less. The posture of both figures is similar: The head, the trunk, and the legs form a different line each. This posture is not a novelty in his work. It can be found also in the sculptures of the Medici Chapel and the figures painted on the ceiling of the Sistine Chapel. These two sculptures for the tomb of Julius II point to the dynamic quality which Michelangelo wished to impart to the representation of the human body. They also have characteristics which set them apart from one another. *Victory* is a young man with a long, slim, body (see p. 76). His left knee leans on the back of a man thrown to the ground who is a symbol for the vanquished. Nevertheless, the young man's demeanor is not that of a triumphant hero rendered arrogant by victory. On the contrary, he stands with his head bent and seems preoccupied by things other than the physical signs of his recent success. His features are calm, meditative. He personifies a victory which is not so much a compelling violence overwhelming the enemy, but rather a victory over man's own impulses, when the latter are pushing him to violence. It is peace over oneself, which is also expressed in *Moses* (see p. 77). The latter is a man in the prime of life, with the body of a giant. His shoulders are wide, his arms muscular. His thick beard flows from his face like the whirling water of a river. Sigmund Freud noted a detail relating to this beard. Moses has just come down from Mount Sinai. He finds out that in his absence the Hebrews have resumed adoring the pagan idol of the Golden Calf. He flies into a violent temper and tries to stand up to call his people to order. The Tables of the Law, which he is holding under his right arm, almost fall

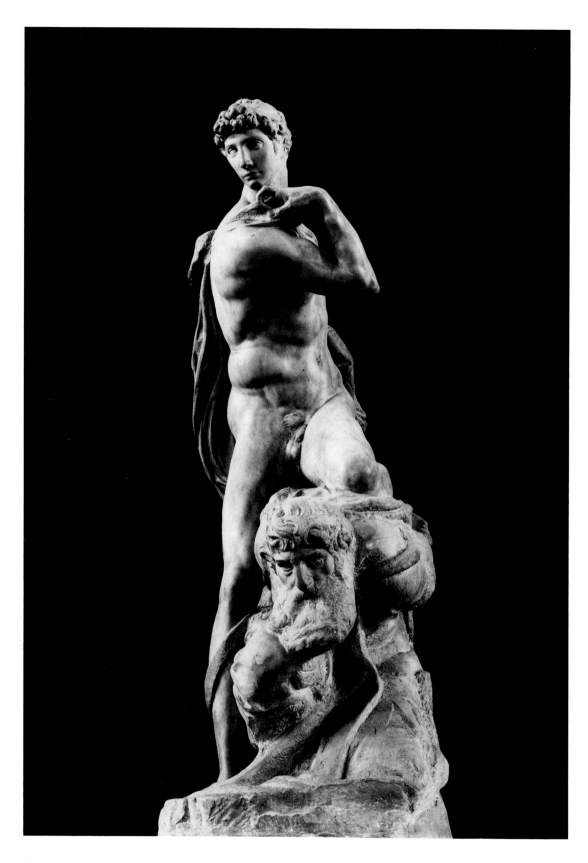

Victory, 1532-1534. Marble, height 102³/₄" (261 cm)
Palazzo della Signoria, Florence. Photo Nicolò Orsi Battaglini, Florence

Moses, ca 1515. Marble carved from 1515 for the tomb of Julius II Height 92 ¹/₂" (235 cm). San Pietro in Vincoli, Rome. Photo Scala, Florence

Pietà, ca 1550. Marble, height 88 ¹⁵/₁₆" (226 cm)
Duomo of Florence. Photo Nicolò Orsi Battaglini, Florence

*Pietà Rondanini. Sculpture left unfinished at the time of Michelangelo's death
Marble, height 76 3/8" (195 cm). Sforza Castle, Milan. Photo Scala, Florence*

down.   He brings his elbow closer to his body, and his index finger leaves a furrow in his flowing beard.   The overall structure of the statue, however, is even more indicative of Michelangelo's principal idea than this detail described by Freud.   Self-control is one component of mental and intellectual strength.   The whole right part of the body, with the arm close to the trunk, creates a strong vertical line.   By contrast, the left side of the prophet, the elbow and the knee in the same oblique motion as the eyes, expresses the violence against which Moses is struggling.   Following the story from the Bible, Michelangelo gave the figure of Moses a meaning which is entirely expressed by this internal tension involving his whole body.   And this is one of his more complete sculptures.

Michelangelo's mind proceeded by weighing opposite forces against one another: *Slaves* tearing themselves from the physical weight of things, *Victory* and *Moses* expressing the domination of the mind over the violent reactions dictated by a desire for power.   In his work, man is neither angel nor beast, but his soul and body are the theater of conflicts.   Man's fate is to confront the physical world as well as his own passions.

Michelangelo had become older and had grown weaker.   In the last fifteen years of his life, he made two sculptures only, a *Pietà* now standing in the cathedral in Florence (see p. 78), and the *Pietà Rondanini*, now in the collection of the Palazzo Sforza in Milan (see p. 79).   The old man had hardly enough strength left for the sculptor's hard work.   He had been on the road all his life, whether to the quarries in Carrara — in order to choose the blocks of marble and have them cut to the size he wanted — or the road between Florence and Rome, going back and forth according to the works he was creating.   He had to climb on scaffoldings when making monumental works.   Finally, he had worked with a hammer and chisel.   He persevered, nevertheless, in spite of his age.   Condivi writes that, six days before he died, Michelangelo was still working on the *Pietà Rondanini*.   The viewer may wonder about these two last works: A mother crying over her dead son expresses traditional Christian commiseration in the face of death.   The word "pietà" in Italian means both piety and pity.   It expresses our worship of the dead, which may alleviate somewhat our grief in the face of the riddle of death.   The *Pietà* in Florence features four figures: Mary and Magdelene are holding the body of Christ, which has surrendered to death.   The tall figure of Nicodemus stands behind Christ.   Vasari claims that his face is a self-portrait.   His presence imparts the sculpture with an upward motion.   The women are holding Christ's body upward, while His legs are collapsing and His head is bent.   Thus, death is not represented as a total defeat.   This body is ready for the Resurrection.   Grief is expressed by the merging of the bodies.   The sculpture is made of polished and rough areas, and this alternate treatment of the stone gives the group a sort of physical unity.   This union beyond death and the hope for a resurrection are even more marked in the *Pietà* which was designed for the mansion of the Rondanini family in Milan (see p. 79).   In this work,

TOMB OF JULIUS II, general view, ca 1515
San Pietro in Vincoli, Rome. Photo Scala, Florence

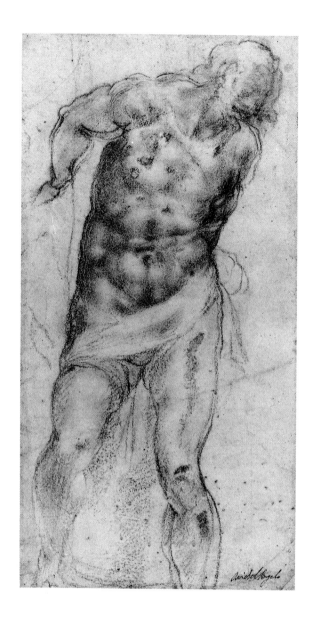

Christ at the Column, undated
Black chalk with some stumping
over stylus overdrawing, heightened with chalk
10 ¹³/₁₆" × 5 ⁵/₈" (27.5 × 14.3 cm)
The British Museum, London. Malcolm Collection

it is unclear whether the mother is holding her son's body upright or whether Christ's body is already caught in the motion which will make Him come out of His tomb three days after His burial, thus making Him support His mother's body. The two bodies are one. Life and death form the whole of man's fate. This was Michelangelo's last thoughts expressed in sculpture. Here again, these ideas are created by the mind's work over form. The mother and her child, the living and the dead, are one because they are united in a single block of stone, the rough surface of which bears everywhere the same chiseled marks.

This was a time when Michelangelo made many drawings, as his hand had become too weak for sculpting. These drawings show a new technique. His earlier drawings both as a young and a mature artist were the drawings of a sculptor, in which he was interested in the strong outlines of articulations and muscles. By contrast, the outline of the bodies in his late drawings are blurred. They are marked by delicate hatching in black chalk, as in the series of drawings on the theme of *Christ on the Cross Between the Virgin and Saint John* (see p. 83) or the moving *Annunciation* in the collection of the Ashmolean Museum in Oxford (see p. 85). The blurred shapes seem almost transparent; the bodies appear to open to the outside and absorb it. The drawing of *The Annunciation* from Oxford may best express Michelangelo's mind at the time. The Virgin and the Angel speak to one another in this airy space because their own body are made of this intangible texture. This technique enabled Michelangelo to describe in drawing a spiritual communion similar to that of the *Pietà Rondanini*, where the Son's body merged with that of His Mother.

Christ on the Cross Between the Virgin and Saint John, ca 1550
Black chalk, 16 ¹/₄" × 11" (41.2 × 27.9 cm). The British Museum, London. Malcolm Collection

The Virgin Annunciate, undated
Black chalk
13 ¹¹/₁₆" × 8 ⁷/₈" (34.8 × 22.4 cm)
The British Museum, London

Michelangelo continued to be very active in his old age, but he worked mainly on architectural designs. The architecture of a building or the layout of an urban area are first designed. Others are then responsible for the actual working site, which requires great physical effort. These were not Michelangelo's first architectural works. In 1515, he had been commissioned by the Pope to design the façade of the San Lorenzo Church in Florence. The same design included also the renovation of the Laurentian Library. At the age of seventy, he worked on new designs for Saint Peter's in Rome, the Piazza del Campidoglio, and the Porta Pia (see p. 86).

In Florence, Michelangelo marked the façade with columns on the lower part of the building, and pilasters on its upper part. The upper part is larger than the lower one, and the upper half of the buildings seems heavier. Michelangelo tried to combine two different principles of architecture. The stability of the building is created by its mass; it weighs heavily on the ground, is rooted in it, so to speak. It is also a building where the structural components are emphasized: The tension between the different parts of the building are made visible by columns, pilasters, arches, entablature, architraves, and cornices. The emphasis on mass is derived from the architecture of ancient Rome. The will to show the balance between the parts is derived from the more recent tradition of Gothic churches, even though Michelangelo's idiom is drawn from the tradition of ancient temples. This combination — and the respective proportions which are given to each part of the building as a result — create such a monumental effect that the design may seem to be too grand for the human scale. Michelangelo, however, was commissioned to create this very monumental effect. Toward the end of his life, the Pope asked him to design the reconstruction of Saint Peter's, the Campidoglio, and the Porta Pia. Saint Peter's (see pp. 88 and 89) and the Campidoglio were completed after he died. Their design is simpler than that of the façade of San Lorenzo and the

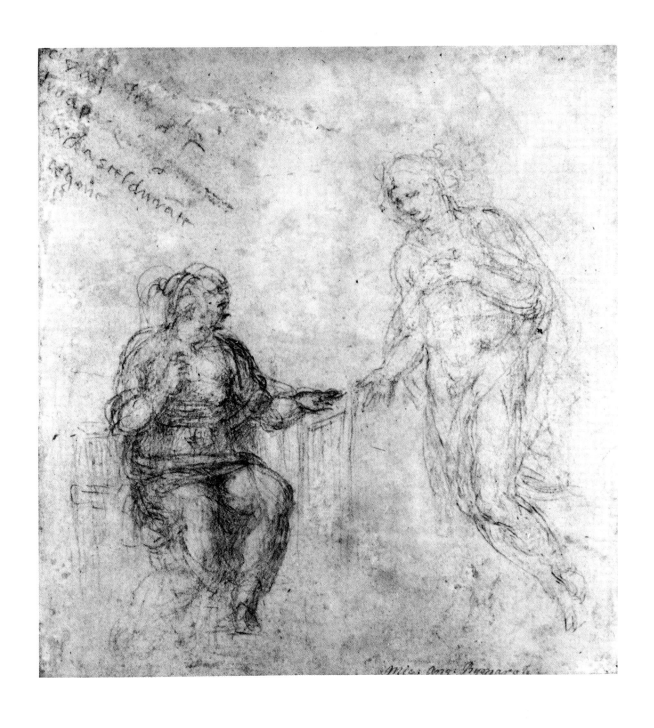

The Annunciation, undated
Black chalk, 87" × 86 5/8" (221 × 220 cm)
The Ashmolean Museum, Oxford

STUDY FOR PORTA PIA
Photo Scala
Florence

Palazzo Farnese, the Façade, Rome, 1546-1549
The third floor and the cornice are by Michelangelo
Photo Scala, Florence

87

The Cupola of the Basilica
Saint Peter's in Rome
Photo Scala, Florence

The Apse of the Basilica
Saint Peter's in Rome, detail
Photo Scala, Florence

Laurentian Library. This very simplification makes them even more monumental. Several architects had been involved in the construction of Saint Peter's before Michelangelo — Sangallo, Bramante, Raphael, and finally Sangallo's son. It proved to be a difficult work. Michelangelo had to suggest several designs to reconcile the constraints created by the site itself, its religious function, its symbolic meaning — especially the meaning of the cupola — and the financial limitations. Saint Peter's design was a remarkable endeavor, in which Michelangelo gave pride of place to the cupola as a symbol of lightness, while the mass of the church was solidly rooted in the ground. Michelangelo as an architect remained the same man who viewed reality as a dynamic clash of forces. The same idea is to be found in his urban designs, the most perfect of which is the Piazza del Campidoglio on Capitoline Hill. The name of the piazza means "the head," the center of the world. Michelangelo made it into a convergence point for all lines of vision. The piazza's pavement outlines an oval shape, which in turn brings to mind the medieval mandorlas, the shape of an almond, the original egg. One side is left open and just edged by a railing. The piazza is closed on the other sides by buildings forming three sides of a trapezium. Thus the convergence of the lines of vision on the center of the piazza is strongly emphasized by an effect of depth of perspective.

Michelangelo's entire work evokes dynamic lines of vision, whether in his urban and architectural designs, his sculptures, or his monumental paintings. They are dynamic lines on a very large scale. The viewer may contrive to consider one of Michelangelo's sculpture as separate from its surroundings and isolated by its installation in a museum, but his sculptures were created with the intention of making them part of a public place. His only paintings were vast decorations celebrating the symbolic meaning of a building, with the sole exception of *The Holy Family* now in the collection of the Uffizi Gallery in Florence, and this is a work of lesser quality. Michelangelo's talent found its accomplishment in vast painted surfaces which were meant to be seen by crowds. As a consequence, his work is dazzling, in every sense of the word. The viewer is made dizzy by the sheer size of Michelangelo's endeavors, his struggle with the broadest expanses of space and the hardest materials, his view of mankind and its fate as a clash of forces. Also, his work marks most clearly a time when the artist's duties were fully social in nature. Nowadays, we may have an ideal view of this harmony between a society and its art. The society which commissioned Michelangelo for works as a sculptor, a painter, an architect, and an urban planner was limited to the powerful. At least, Michelangelo was on an equal footing with the powerful, or almost equal. His relationship with the Pope was marked by stormy clashes and he was never reduced — as artists often were in the course of history — to being a mere provider of small pleasures for the rich and of entertainment for the crowds. We may have an idealized notion of these times, which must have often been difficult for artists, but at least we are cherishing a noble nostalgia.

MARC LE BOT

BIOGRAPHY

1475   Michelangelo Buonarroti was born on March 6, at Caprese. His father, Ludovico, was the city's "podestà."

1481   His mother died.

1488   Entered the studio of Domenico Ghirlandajo in Florence. He studied sculpture at the Giardino Mediceo under Bertoldo di Giovanni, a student af Donatello.

1490-1492 Lived in the palace of his patron, Lorenzo de Medici. Carved the marble reliefs of the *Madonna of the Stairs* and *Battle of the Centaurs*.

1492   Lorenzo de Medici died in April. Michelangelo returned to his father's house.

1492-1494 Executed a wooden *Crucifixion* and a statue of Hercules.

1494   Fleeing from political unrest in Florence, he left on October 14. After a brief visit to Venice, he stayed for a year in Bologna. There, he executed three small sculptures and acquainted himself with the writings of Dante, Petrarch, and Boccaccio.

1495   Returned to Florence, where he did two statues, *San Giovannino* and *Sleeping Cupid*.

1496-1501 First stay in Rome, where he was the protégé of Cardinal Riario and Cardinal Bilhères. He did the marble *Pietà* of St. Peter's and a *Bacchus*.

1501-1505 Returned to Florence, where he was commissioned to do the marble *David* and *Bruges Madonna*. He was also commissioned to design a fresco depicting the Battle of Cascina, which was to decorate a wall of the council hall in the Palazzo della Signoria. Leonardo da Vinci was supposed to paint a fresco of *The Battle of Anghiari* on the opposite wall.

1505   Returned to Rome, where he started work on the sepulchral monument of Pope Julius II.

1506   Julius II abandoned his plans for a tomb. Michelangelo was offended and he fled to Florence on August 17. Their breach was healed in November and he returned to Rome.

1508-1512 Worked on the decoration of the ceiling of the Sistine Chapel.

1513   Leon X succeeded Julius II. Second design for the monumental tomb of Julius II. Executed the *Rebellious Slave* and *Dying Slave*.

1516   Third design for the tomb of Julius II. Leon X commissioned Michelangelo for the façade of San Lorenzo in Florence. He left for Florence and made frequent trips to the marble quarries in Carrara.

1519   *The Risen Christ.*

1520-1527 Worked on the Medici Chapel in San Lorenzo, in Florence.

1527   The troops of Holy Roman Emperor Charles V captured and sacked Rome in May. Second revolution in Florence. A republican regime was established. Michelangelo assisted as engineer in the defense of Florence.

1529   Fearing the political developments in Florence, Michelangelo fled to Ferrara, and then to Venice. He came back to Florence in November and resumed work on the fortification walls. He went into hiding after Florence was defeated by the Pope's army.

1530   Pardoned by Pope Clement VII in August.

1530-1534 Resumed work on the Medici Chapel in Florence.

1532   Met Tommaso Cavalieri. Wrote many poems.

1534   Settled in Rome. Paul III succeeded Clement VII and had Michelangelo continue to decorate the Sistine Chapel. *The Last Judgment*. Friendship with Vittoria Colonna, who belonged to a movement for a spiritual reformation within the Catholic Church.

1542-1545 Completed the monumental tomb of Julius II and painted the frescoes of the Pauline Chapel.

1546   Completed the Palazzo Farnese. Worked on the Piazza del Campidoglio on Capitoline Hill and became chief architect of St. Peter's Church.

1550   Julius III succeeded Paul III. Michelangelo did the Florence *Pietà*.

1555   Paul IV succeeded Julius III. Michelangelo started work on the *Pietà Rondanini*.

1559   Pius IV succeeded Paul IV. Michelangelo worked on Porta Pia.

1564   Michelangelo died on February 14.

BIBLIOGRAPHY

WRITINGS BY MICHELANGELO, LETTERS AND POEMS

Le Lettere de Michelangelo Buonarroti. Ed. by Gaetano Milanesi. Florence: Le Monnier, 1875.

Lettres de Michel-Ange. Trans. by Marie Dormy. Paris: Rieder, 1926.

Die Briefe des Michelangiolo Buonarroti. Trans. by Karl Frey. 3rd ed. with notes by Herman Walther Frey. Berlin: Walter de Gruyter, 1961.

The Letters of Michelangelo. Trans. and notes by E.H. Ramsden. 2 vols. London: Peter Owen; Stanford, Cal.: Stanford University Press, 1963.

Il Carteggio di Michelangelo. Ed. by Giovanni Poggi, Paola Barocchi and Renzo Ristori. 5 vols. Florence: Sansoni, 1965-1983.

Le Rime de Michelangelo Buonarrotti. Ed. by Cesare Guasti. Florence: Le Monnier, 1863.

Michelangiolo. Rime. Ed. by Giovanni Papini. Florence: Rinascimento del libro, 1927.

Michelangelo. The Complete Poems. Ed. by Joseph Tusiani. New York: Noonday Press, 1960.

Rime. Ed. by E.N. Girardi. Bari: Laterza, 1960.

Sonnets. Trans. by Georges Ribemont. Paris: Club français du Livre, 1961.

Poèmes. Illustrated with 35 drawings. Ed. by Pierre Leyris. Paris: Mazarine, 1984.

I Ricordi. Ed. by L. Bardeschi Ciulich and P. Barocchi. Florence: Sansoni, 1970.

BOOKS ON MICHELANGELO, HIS LIFE, HIS WORK, AND HIS TIME

ALEXANDER, Sidney. *Michelangelo, il Fiorentino.* Milan: Martello, 1959.

BECK, James. *Michelangelo. A Lesson in Anatomy.* London: Phaidon, 1975.

BERENCE, Fred. *Michel-Ange ou la volonté de puissance.* Paris: La Colombe, 1947.

BERNARD, Émile. *Le grand et très divin Michel-Ange. Étude esthétique de l'homme et de l'œuvre.* Tonnerre: M.A. Bernard, 1924.

BERTI, Luciano. *Michelangelo.* Florence, 1968.

BERTINI, Aldo. *Michelangelo fino alla Sistina.* 2nd ed. Turin: Einaudi, 1945.

BIRNI, Walter. *Michelangelo scrittore.* Turin: Einaudi, 1975.

BLACK, Charles Christopher. *Michel Angelo Buonarroti, Sculptor, Painter, Architect. The Story of His Life and Labours.* London: Macmillan, 1875.

BOSCO, Umberto. *Il Rinascimento e la lirica di Michelangelo.* Rome: De Santis, 1960-1961.

BRANDES, G.M.C. *Michelangelo, His Life, His Time, His Era.* Trans. and foreword by Heinz Norden. London: Constable; New York: Ungar, 1963.

CALI, M. *Da Michelangelo all'Escorial.* Turin, 1980.

CEMÓN AZNAR, José. *Miguel Angel.* Madrid: Espasa-Calpe, 1975.

CLEMENTS, Robert J. *Michelangelo's Theory of Art.* New York: Gramercy Publishing Co., 1961.

CLEMENTS, Robert J. *Michelangelo. A Self-Portrait.* Englewood Cliffs, N.J.: Prentice-Hall, 1963.

CLEMENTS, Robert J. *The Poetry of Michelangelo.* New York: New York University Press, 1965.

CONDIVI, Ascanio. *La Vita de Michel Angelo Buonarroti.* Florence: Gaetano Albizzini, 1746.

D'ANCONA, P., PINNA, A., CARDELLINI, I. *Michelangelo. Architettura, pittura, scultura.* With *La Vita de Michel Angelo Buonarroti* by Ascanio Condivi. Milan: Bramante, 1964.

DELOGU, C. *Michelangiolo. Bildhauer, Maler, Architekt.* Zurich: Fretz and Wasmuth, 1939.

DE MAIO, R. *Michelangelo e la Controriforma.* Bari, 1978, 1981.

EINEM, Herbert von. *Michelangiolo. Bilhauer, Maler, Baumeister.* Berlin: Gebr.-Mann, 1973.

FREY, Dagobert. *Michelangiolo Studien.* Vienna: Schroll, 1920.

FREY, Karl. *Michelangiolo Buonarroti. Sein Leben und seine Werke.* Berlin: K. Curtius, 1907.

FROMMEL, Christoph Luitpold. *Michelangelo and Tommaso dei Cavalieri.* Amsterdam: Castrum Peregrini Presse, 1979.

GOLDSCHEIDER, Ludwig. *Michelangiolo. Gemälde, Skulpturen, Architekuren.* Cologne: Phaidon, 1953, 1954, 1956, 1959.

GOTTI, Aurelio. *Vita de Michelangiolo Buonarroti.* 2 vols. 2nd ed., Florence: Gazzetta d'Italia, 1876.

GRIMM, Hermann. *Leben Michelangiolos.* Vienna, Leipzig: Phaidon, 1901. Complete ed., Leipzig: Dietrich, 1940.

HARFORD, John S. *The Life of Michael Angelo Buonarroti.* London: Longman, Brown and Green, 1857.

HIBBARD, Howard. *Michelangelo.* Harmondsworth: Pelican Books, 1975.

ISPER, Karl. *Michelangiolo, Künstler und Prophet.* Regensburg: Pustet, 1977.

LACRETELLE, Jacques de, ed. *Michel-Ange.* Paris: Hachette, 1961.

LIEBERT, Robert. *Michelangelo: A Psychoanalytic Study of His Life and Images*. New Haven, Conn., London: Yale University Press, 1983.

MARIANI, Valerio. *Michelangelo*. Turin, Naples: Libreria scientifica, 1942. New revised edition, 1964.

MARIANI, Valerio. *Leonardo e Michelangelo*. Naples: Libreria scientifica, 1965.

MARNAT, Marcel. *Michel-Ange, une vie*. Paris: Gallimard, 1974.

MUCHNIK, Mario. *Michel-Ange de près*. Int. by Anthony Burgess. Trans. by Laure Guille-Bataillon. Paris: Laffont, 1975.

MURRAY, Linda. *Michelangelo, His Life, Work and Times*. London: Thames and Hudson, 1984.

PAPINI, Giovanni. *Vita di Michelangiolo nella vita del suo tempo*. Milan: Garzanti, 1949; Mondadori, 1964.

PARRONCHI, Alessandro. *Opere giovanili di Michelangelo*. Florence: Olschki, 1968-1981.

PERRIG, Alexandra. *Michelangiolo Studien*. 5 vols. Frankfurt: Peter Lang; Bern: Herbert Lang, 1976.

RECUPERO, Jacopo. *Michelangelo*. Rome: De Luca, 1965.

RICCI, R. *Michel-Ange*. Florence, 1902.

RIVOSECCHI, Mario. *Michelangelo e Roma*. Bologna: Cappelli, 1965.

ROLLAND, Romain. *Michel-Ange*. With *Lettres, poésies et témoignages*. Ed. by André Chastel. Paris: Albin Michel, 1958.

SALVINI, Roberto. *Michelangelo*. Milan, 1977.

SCHINNERER, Adolf. *Michelangiolo's Weltgericht*. Munich: Piper, 1949.

SCHOTT, Rolf. *Michelangiolo. Der Mensch und sein Werk*. Gütersloh: Bertelsmann, 1962.

STEINMANN, Ernst. *Michelangiolo im Spiegel seiner Zeit*. Leipzig, 1930.

SYMONDS, John Addington. *The Life of Michelangelo Buonarroti Based on Studies in the Archives of the Buanarroti Family in Florence*. 2 vols. London, 1893.

THODE, Henry. *Michelangiolo. Kritische Untersuchung über seine Werke*. 3 vols. Berlin: Grote, 1908-1913.

THODE, Henry. *Michelangiolo und das Ende der Renaissance*. 4 vols. Berlin: Grote, 1902-1912.

TOLNAY, Charles de. *Michelangelo*. 5 vols. Princeton, N.J.: Princeton University Press, 1947-1960.

TOLNAY, Charles de. *Werk und Weltbild des Michelangelo*. Zurich: Rhein, 1949.

TOLNAY, Charles de. *Michel-Ange*. Paris: Tisné, 1951.

TOLNAY, Charles de. *Michel-Ange*. Paris: Flammarion, 1970.

TOLNAY, Charles de, BALDINI, Umberto, SALVINI, Roberto, DE ANGELIS D'OSSAT, Guglielmo. *Michelangelo, artista, pensatore, scrittore*. 2 vols. Novara: Agostini, 1965.

NUDE FIGURE NEXT TO THE SCENE
OF NOAH'S SACRIFICE, 1509
Fresco
Musei del Vaticano, Sistine Chapel, The Vault
Photo P. Zigrossi

TOLNAY, Charles de, GOSEBRUCH, Martin, DUSSLER, Luitpold, HUBALA, Erich. *Michelangelo Buonarroti.* Würzburg: Leonhardt, 1964.

TOLNAY, Charles de, and SQUELLATI BRIZZIO, P. *Michelangelo e i Medici.* Florence, 1980.

VASARI, Giorgio. *La Vita de Michelangelo nelle redazioni del 1550 e del 1568.* Ed. and biblio. by Paola Barocchi. 5 vols. Milan, Naples: Ricciardi, 1962.

VASARI, Giorgio. *The Great Masters: Giotto, Botticelli, Leonardo, Raphael, Michelangelo, Titian.* Trans. by Gaston de Vere. Ed. by Michael Sonino. New York: Lauter and Levin, 1986.

WILDE, Johannes. *Michelangelo. Six Lectures.* Oxford: Clarendon Press, 1978.

WILSON. *Life and Works of Michelangelo.* London, 1876

MICHELANGELO THE SCULPTOR

CATALOGUES RAISONNÉS

BALDINI, Umberto, ed. *L'Opera completa di Michelangelo scultore.* Milan: Rizzoli, 1973.

GOLDSCHEIDER, Ludwig. *A Survey of Michelangelo's Models in Wax and Clay.* London: Phaidon, 1962.

HARTT, Frederick. *Michelangelo. The Complete Sculpture.* New York: Abrams, 1968. London: Thames and Hudson, 1969.

RUSSOLI, Franco. *Tutta la scultura di Michelangelo.* Milan: Rizzoli, 1953, 1959, 1962.

BOOKS ON SCULPTURES BY MICHELANGELO

ALAZARD, Jean. *Les Sculptures de Michel-Ange.* Paris: Hazan, 1949.

BALDINI, Umberto. *Michelangelo scultore.* Florence: Sansoni, 1981.

BATTISTI, Eugenio. *Les Sculptures de Michel-Ange.* Trans. by L. Chanteloup. Paris: Atlas, 1983.

DE' MAFFEI, Fernanda. *Michelangelo's Lost St. John. The Story of a Discovery.* London: Faber; New York: Reynal, 1964.

GOLDSCHEIDER, Ludwig. *The Sculpture of Michelangelo.* London: Phaidon, 1939, 1950.

GUAZZONI, Valerio. *Michel-Ange sculpteur.* Paris: Cercle d'art, 1984.

HARTT, Frederick. *David by the Hand of Michelangelo. The Original Model Discovered.* London: Thames and Hudson, 1987.

LAUX, Karl. *Michelangiolos Julius. Monument.* Berlin: Ebering, 1943.

LE BROOY, P.J. *Michelangelo. Models formerly in the Paul von Praun Collection.* Vancouver: Greelman and Drummond, 1972.

MALLARMÉ, Camille. *Un Drame ignoré de Michel-Ange.* Paris: F. Didot, 1930.

MANCUSI-UNGARO, Harold R., *Michelangelo. The Bruges Madonna and the Piccolomini Altar.* New Haven, London: Yale University Press, 1971.

PANOFSKY, Erwin. *Tomb Sculpture.* New York: Abrams, 1964.

POPE, Henessy. *Italian High Renaissance and Baroque Sculpture.* London: Phaidon, 1963.

POPP, A.E. *Die Medici Kapelle Michelangelos.* Munich, 1922.

WEINBERGER, Martin. *Michelangelo the Sculptor.* 2 vols. London: Routledge and Kegan; New York: Columbia University Press, 1967.

MICHELANGELO AS A PAINTER

CATALOGUE RAISONNÉ

TOLNAY, Charles de. *Tout l'œuvre peint de Michel-Ange.* Documentation by Ettore Camesasca. Paris: Flammarion, 1967, 1986.

BOOKS ON PAINTINGS BY MICHELANGELO

BATTISTI, E. *La Cappella Sistina.* Novara: Agostini, 1983.

BOYER D'AGEN. *Michel-Ange: le plafond de la Sixtine, le Jugement dernier.* Paris, 1931-1934.

CHASTEL, A. *The Vatican Frescoes of Michelangelo.* New York, 1980.

DE VECCHI, Pier Luigi. *Michel-Ange peintre.* Paris: Cercle d'art, 1984.

D'ANCONA, P. *Affreschi della Cappella Paolina.* Milan, 1952.

DE CAMPOS. *Affreschi della Cappella Paolina.* Milan, 1951.

ETTLINGER, L.D. *The Sistine Chapel before Michelangelo: Religious Imagery and Papal Primacy.* Oxford, 1965.

FREEDBERG, S.J. *Circa 1600: A Revolution of Style in Italian Painting.* Cambridge, Mass., London: Harvard University Press, 1983.

HAUSSHERR, R. *Michelangelos Krucifixus für Vittoria Colonna: Bemerkungen zur Ikonographie und theologischer Deutung.* Opladen, 1971.

JOHN, R. *Dante und Michelangelo: Das Paradiso terrestre und die sixtinische Decke.* Krefeld, 1959.

MARIANI, V. *Gli affreschi di Michelangelo nella Cappella Paolina.* Rome, 1932.

PANOFSKY, E. *Die sixtinische Decke.* Leipzig, 1921.

RAGGHIANTI, L. *La Cappella Sistina in Vaticano.* Milan, 1965.

REDIG DE CAMPOS. *Michel-Ange, les fresques de la chapelle Pauline au Vatican.* Milan, 1952.

SALINGER, M. *The Last Judgment.* New York, 1965.

SANDSTROM, S. *The Sistine Chapel Ceiling, in Levels of Unreality: Studies in Structure and Construction in Italian Mural Painting During the Renaissance.* Stockholm, 1963.

SEYMOUR, C. Jr. *Michelangelo: The Sistine Chapel Ceiling.* London, 1972.

STEINBERG, L. *Michelangelo's Last Paintings.* London, 1975.

STEINMANN, E. *Die Sixtinische Kapelle.* Munich, 1901-1905.

WILDE, J. *The Decoration of the Sistine Chapel.* London, 1958.

MICHELANGELO AS AN ARCHITECT

CATALOGUE RAISONNÉ

ARGO, G.C., BERTINI, A., BETTINI, S., BONELLI, R., GIOSEFFI, D., PANE, R., PORTOGHESI, P., ZEVI, B. *Michelangiolo architetto.* Catalogue of the complete work by Franco Barbieri and Lionello Puppi. Notes by Paolo Portoghesi and Bruno Zevi. Turin: Einaudi, 1964.

BOOKS ON THE ARCHITECTURE DESIGNED BY MICHELANGELO

ACKERMAN, J.S. *The Architecture of Michelangelo.* London, 1961.

GEYMÜLLER, Heinrich von. *Michelangelo Buonarroti als Architekt: Nach neuen Quellen.* Munich, 1904.

NOVA, Alessandro. *Michel-Ange architecte.* Paris: Cercle d'art, 1984.

SCHIAVO, Armando. *La Vita e le opere architettoniche di Michelangelo.* Rome: Libreria dello stato, 1953.

ZEVI, Bruno, ed.. *Michelangiolo architetto. Michelangelo as architect.* Milan: ETAS/KOMPASS, 1964. Reprint of the January 1964 issue (no. 99) of the journal "L'Architettura, Cronacha e Storia".

DRAWINGS BY MICHELANGELO

CATALOGUES RAISONNÉS

DUSSLER, Luitpold. *Die Zeichnungen des Michelangiolos. Kritischer Katalog.* Berlin: Gebr-Mann, 1959.

FREY, Karl, ed. *Die Handzeichnungen Michelangiolo Buonarroti: Herausgegeben und mit kritischen Apparate versehen.* 3 vols. Berlin: J. Bard, 1909-1911.

TOLNAY, Charles de. *Corpus dei disegni di Michelangelo.* 4 vols. Novara: Agostini, 1975-1980.

BOOKS ON DRAWINGS BY MICHELANGELO

BAROCCHI, Paola. *Michelangelo e sua scuola. I disegni di Casa Buonarroti e degli Uffizi.* 3 vols. Florence: Olschki, 1962-1964.

BRINCKMANN, A.E. *Michelangelo-Zeichnungen.* Munich, 1925.

DAL POGGETTO, Paolo. *I Disegni murali di Michelangelo e della sua scuola nella Sagrestia nuova di San Lorenzo.* Florence: Centro Di, 1978.

DELACRE, Maurice. *Le Dessin de Michel-Ange.* Thesis for the Académie royale de Belgique, Brussels, 1938.

GOLDSCHEIDER, Ludwig. *Michelangelo. Drawings.* London: Phaidon, 1951. 2nd revised ed. London: Phaidon; Greenwich, Conn.: New York Graphic Society, 1966.

HARTT, Frederick. *The Drawings of Michelangelo.* London: Thames and Hudson, 1971.

MARCUARD, F. von. *Die Zeichnungen Michelangiolos in Museum Teyler zu Haarlem.* Munich: Bruckmann, 1901.

MAURENBRECHER, Wolf. *Die Aufzeichnungen des Michelangiolo Buonarroti im Britischen Museum in London und im Vermächtnis Ernst Steinmann in Rom.* Leipzig: H. Keller, 1938.

PREISS, Pavel. *Michel-Ange. Dessins.* Paris: Cercle d'art, 1976.

ROBINSON, J.C. *A Critical Account of the Drawings by Michel Angelo and Raffaello in the University Galleries, Oxford.* Oxford, 1870.

WILDE, Johannes. *Italian Drawings in the Department of Prints and Drawings in the British Museum. Michelangelo and His Studio.* London: British Museum, 1952.

EXHIBITIONS

1964 *Michelangelo. Disegni, manoscritti e documenti.* Casa Buonarroti and Biblioteca Laurenziana, Florence.

1975 *Drawings by Michelangelo in the collection of her Majesty the Queen at Windsor Castle, the Ashmolean Museum, the British Museum and other English collections.* British Museum, London. Int. by J.A. Gere.

1975 *Michelangiolo Buonarroti e il Veneto.* Università degli studi, Padua. Cat. by Paolo Carpeggiani.

1975-1976 *Disegni di Michelangelo nelle collezioni italiane.* Casa Buonarroti, Galleria degli Uffizi, Florence. Cat. by Charles de Tolnay.

1979 *Drawings by Michelangelo from the British Museum.* The Pierpont Morgan Library, New York. Cat. by J.A. Gere.

1980 *Michelangelo e i Medici.* Casa Buonarroti, Florence. Notes by Charles de Tolnay and Paolo Squellati Brizzio.

1984 *Raffaello e Michelangelo.* Casa Buonarroti, Florence. Cat. by Anna Forlani Tempesti.

1985 *Michelangelo e i maestri del Quattrocento.* Casa Buonarroti, Florence. Cat. by Carli Sisi.

1987 *Michelangelo e l'arte classica.* Casa Buonarroti, Florence. Cat. by Giovanni Agosti and Vincenzo Farinella.

1988-1989 *Drawings by Michelangelo.* National Gallery of Art, Washington, D.C.; Musée du Louvre, Paris. Cat. by Michael Hirst.

ILLUSTRATIONS